Crochet Variations

Margaret Wilkes

Dryad Press Ltd, London

Acknowledgement

I would like to express my sincere thanks to all the wonderful people who have assisted me with the production of this book. I especially wish to thank Pem Harper, who tests all my patterns, for her dedication and encouragement: Joan Morgan, my close friend and companion on many field trips, who does all my typing. Thanks also go to illustrators Graham and Karen Morgan; photographer Dave Clarke; models Lee Davies, Karen Mitchell, Benjamin Wallace, Julia Ball and my grandchildren Phillip, John, and Clair Wilkes. David Jackson for his help with this text; Roger Underhill for the bridal flowers: Colin Penn and the staff of Chanteleine, France; Clive Royston and all my friends at George Picaud et Cie in Paris and the many others involved in the making of this book.

Photographs by Dave Clarke
Drawings by Karen Elizabeth Morgan

ISBN 0 8521 9633 4

Typeset by Tek-Art Ltd, Kent
and printed in Great Britain by
Anchor Brendon Ltd
Tiptree, Essex
for the publishers
Dryad Press Ltd
4 Fitzhardinge Street
London W1H 0AH

Contents

Abbreviations *4*
Equipment *5*
   Tools
   Crochet hooks
Introduction *6*

1. Basic stitches *7*
   Slip stitch
   Double crochet
   Half treble
   Treble crochet
   Rounds of double crochet

The Projects

2. V-neck pullover *14*
3. Waistcoat *15*
   Squares
   Triangles
4. Party top *20*
5. Evening bag *23*
6. Jumper *24*
   Cross treble stitch
7. Short sleeve alpaca
   jumper *27*
   Shell stitch
8. Ribbed cotton boob
   tube *30*
   Rib stitch

9. Family ribbed sweater *32*
10. Ribbed hat *35*
11. Ribbed scarf *37*
   Fringe
12. Necklace *38*
13. Bracelet *40*
14. Wedding dress *41*
15. Bridesmaids' dresses *45*
   Broomstick skirt and sleeves
16. Cotton bag *50*
   Broomstick stitch
17. Cushion cover *52*
   Tunisian stitch
18. Tunisian rug *54*
19. Coat *56*
20. Hat *59*
21. Tunisian bluebell top *60*
   Tunisian framed squares
22. Ironbridge Tunisian
   top *63*
23. Ironbridge Tunisian
   sweater *66*
24. Tunisian sweater and
   top *69*

Suppliers *71*

Abbreviations

slip stitch	ss
chain(s)	ch(s)
double crochet	dc
half treble(s)	hlf tr(s)
treble(s)	tr(s)
yarn round hook	yrh
yarn over hook	yoh
loop(s)	lp(s)
round(s)	rnd(s)
stitch	st
stiches	sts
increase	in
decrease	dec
number	no
pattern	patt
repeat	rep
space	sp
beginning	beg
centimetre	cm
inch	in
alternative	alt
together	tog
cross stitch	cr st
Tunisian stitch	Ts
cross treble	cr tr
treble front	tr fr
treble back	tr bk

Equipment

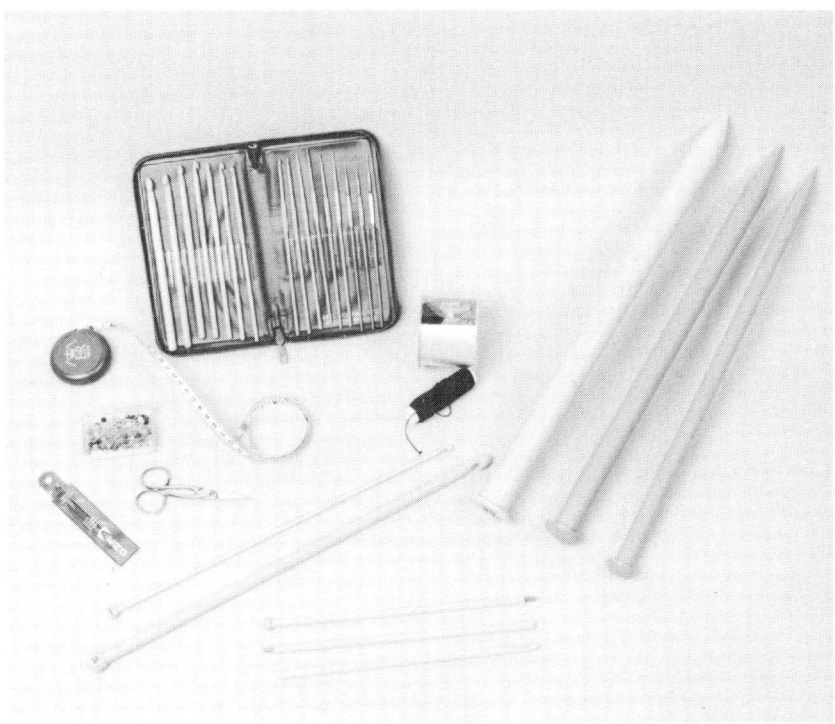

Tools	Crochet hooks	
crochet hook	Old size	New size
25mm pin	2	7.00
20mm pin	4	6.00
15mm pin	5	5.50
sectional blanket hook (3 pieces)	6	5.00
10mm Tunisian crochet hook	7	4.50
5.00 Tunisian crochet hook	8	4.00
tape measure	9	3.50
scissors	10	3.00
wool sewing needles	12	2.50
pins	14	2.00
knitting elastic		

Introduction

All my life I've been craft-minded. I have dabbled in painting and tapestry and rug-making and, over the years, must have knitted up enough yarn to reach to the moon and back.

My interest in crochet began to develop in 1969 when I realised the speed and economy with which garments could be produced using just one simple tool. I was delighted to discover the huge variety of patterns, stitches and designs that were possible and surprised by the ease with which I progressed from the simple stitches to the more complicated sort. Going from strength to strength I quickly began inventing stitches and designing patterns of my own.

Before long my ideas were being published in national magazines and I was teaching and demonstrating crochet on a regular basis around Great Britain and in Europe.

In 1978 at the Intersew Exhibition in Monte Carlo I had the honour of meeting and demonstrating my technique to Princess Caroline of Monaco. The following year, while demonstrating Broomstick crochet for Aero and the needle manufacturers, I was presented to Princess Caroline's mother, the late Princess Grace, who showed great interest in my work. This encounter was broadcast on Monaco television news. I have also appeared with Jean Morton on the British television programme *Women Today*.

My purpose in mentioning these small triumphs is to demonstrate how quickly one can move from being a beginner to becoming an accomplished expert and discover how very rewarding and exciting this craft can be.

This, my fourth crochet publication, is intended to be both a primer for the absolute novice and a project source book for those already competant in the craft.

If you are just starting to crochet I hope that you too will enjoy the same success in your efforts and derive an equal amount of pleasure and satisfaction from this fascinating craft. As for the more accomplished reader I hope that you will find many challenging new ideas and original designs with which to experiment.

1. The Basic Stitches

Slip stitch

This is the st used to dec, which slips along a row or joins rnds.
Insert the hook into the first st, thread over the hook and draw through two lps, one movement, 1 ss is completed.
To inc, work two sts into one st, or make an extra ch st or sts at the beg or end of the work.

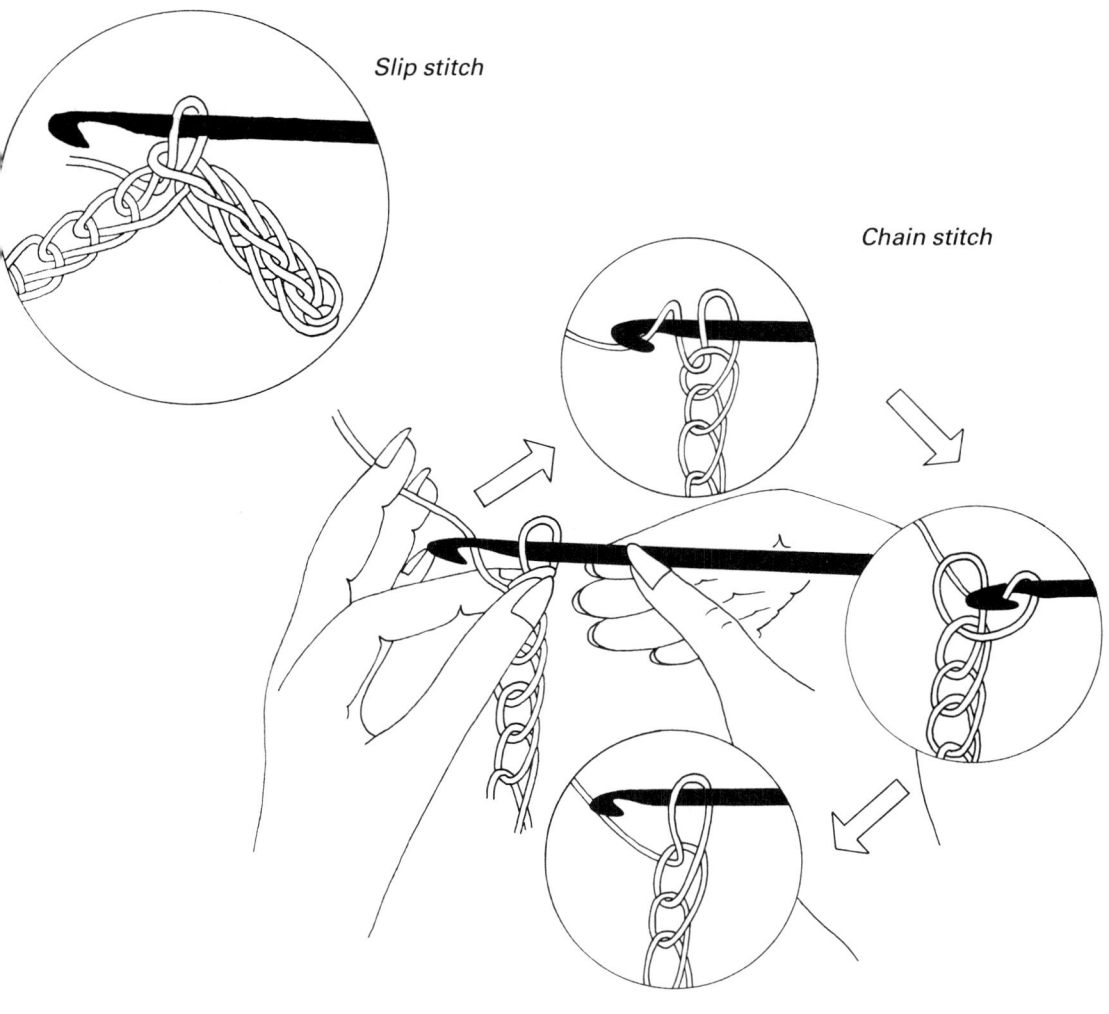

Slip stitch

Chain stitch

Double crochet

Materials

With a 4.00 crochet hook and DK yarn make 20 ch.
Row 1 Insert the hook under the 2 top threads of 2 ch from the hook.
Yarn over the hook (yoh), towards you.

Draw the thread through the ch (there are 2 lps on the hook).

Thread over the hook and draw through 2 lps (1 lp on the hook). 1 dc
is completed.

For the next dc insert the hook under the 2 top threads of the next ch
and rep as the last ch.

Rep dc into each of the top 2 lps, which is 1 st into each ch to the end
of the row. *1 ch to turn.*
Row 2 1 dc into the first 2 top lps, and into each st to end of row, making
sure, the last st is 2 top lps. *1 ch to turn.* Rep 2nd row to length required.
Note To fasten off, clip the thread from the work, bring the end through
the rem lp and pull.

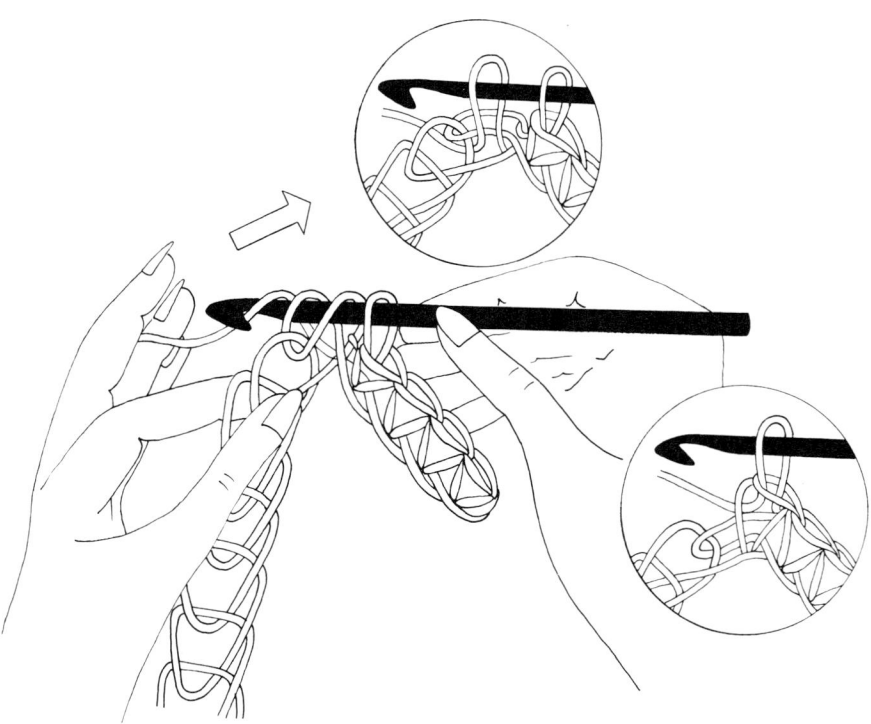

Half treble

Materials

With 4.00 crochet hook and DK yarn make 20 ch.

Row 1 Insert hook under, thread towards you. Insert hook into 3rd ch from hook. Thread over hook and pull through ch (3 lps on hook). Thread over hook, draw through all lps on hook (1 lp on hook) 1 hlf tr is completed. Rep hlf tr into each ch to end of row. *2 ch to turn.*

Row 2 1 hlf tr into each 2 top lps, remember to go into first 2 top lps and the last two top lps. *2 ch to turn.*

Rep 2nd row to length required. Fasten off.

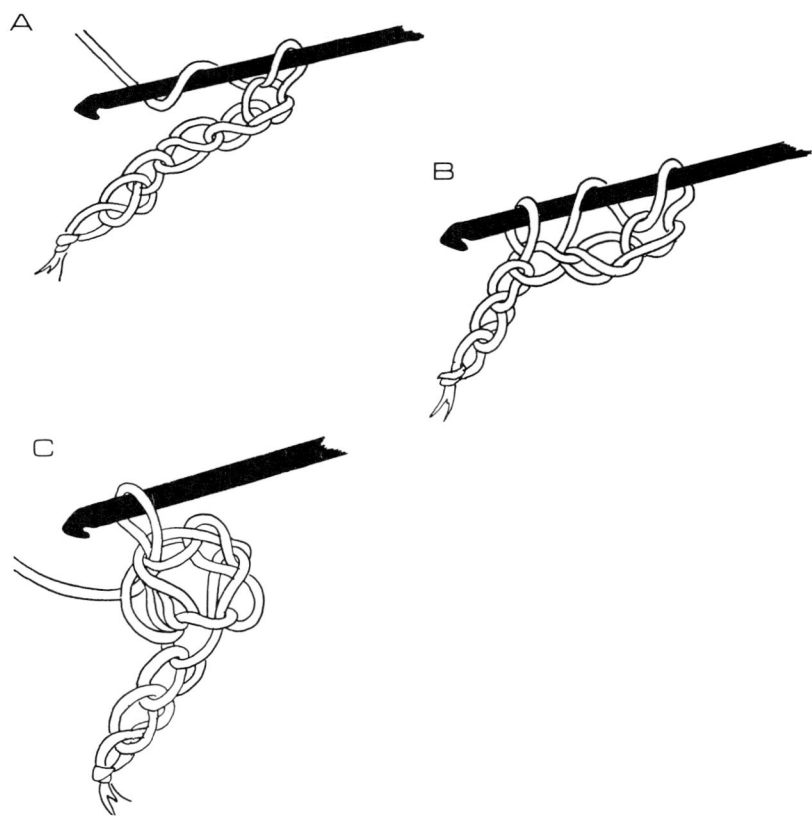

Treble crochet

Materials

With a 4.00 crochet hook and DK yarn make 20 ch.

Row 1 Insert hook under, thread towards you. Insert hook into 3rd ch from hook. Thread over hook, and draw through st (3 lps on hook). Thread over hook, and draw through 2 lps (2 lps on hook). Thread over hook, and draw through 2 lps (1 lp on hook).

1 tr is completed.

Rep tr into each ch to end of row. *2 ch to turn.*

Row 2 Tr into first 2 top lps, then in each st and last 2 top lps, *2 ch to turn.*

Rep 2nd row until length required. Fasten off.

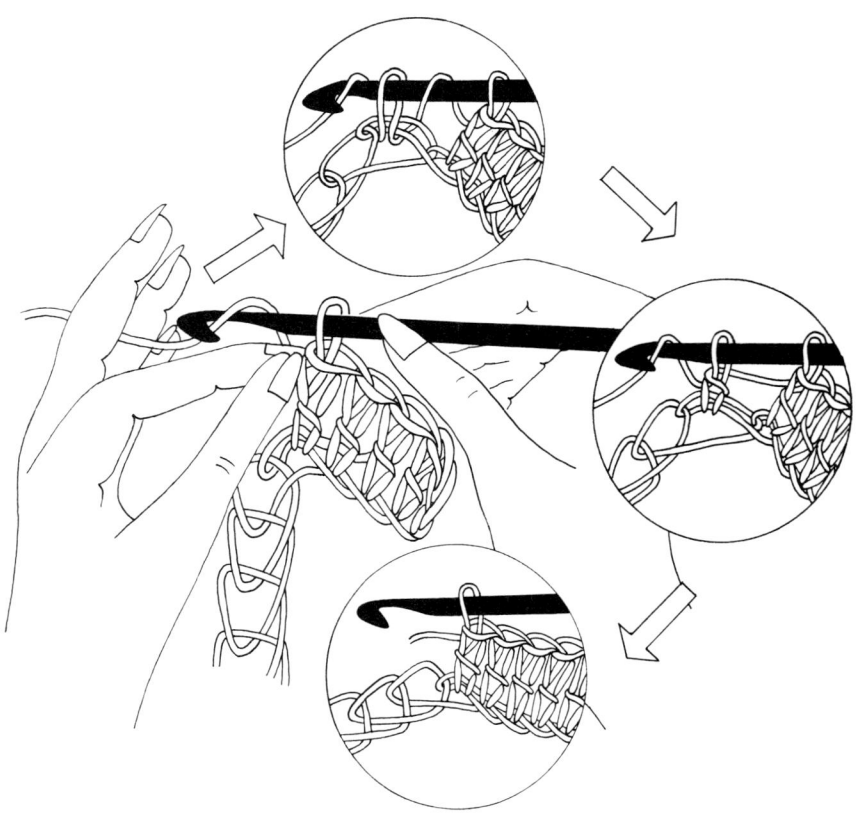

Rounds of double crochet

Materials

With 4.00 crochet hook and DK yarn, make 5 ch. Join with a ss to first ch st to form a ring.

Rnd 1 1 ch, make 10 dc into ring, ss to first dc, place a safety pin to mark the end of a rnd, move the safety pin to mark each rnd.

Rnd 2 1 ch, 2 dc in each dc (20 dc), ss to first dc.

Rnd 3 *(2 dc in next 1 dc, 1 dc in next dc.) Rep from * to end of rnd. Ss to first dc.

Rnd 4 1 ch *(1 dc in next 2 dc, 2 dc in next dc). Rep from * to end of rnd. Ss to first dc.

   To fasten off the next st pull the thread through the lp.

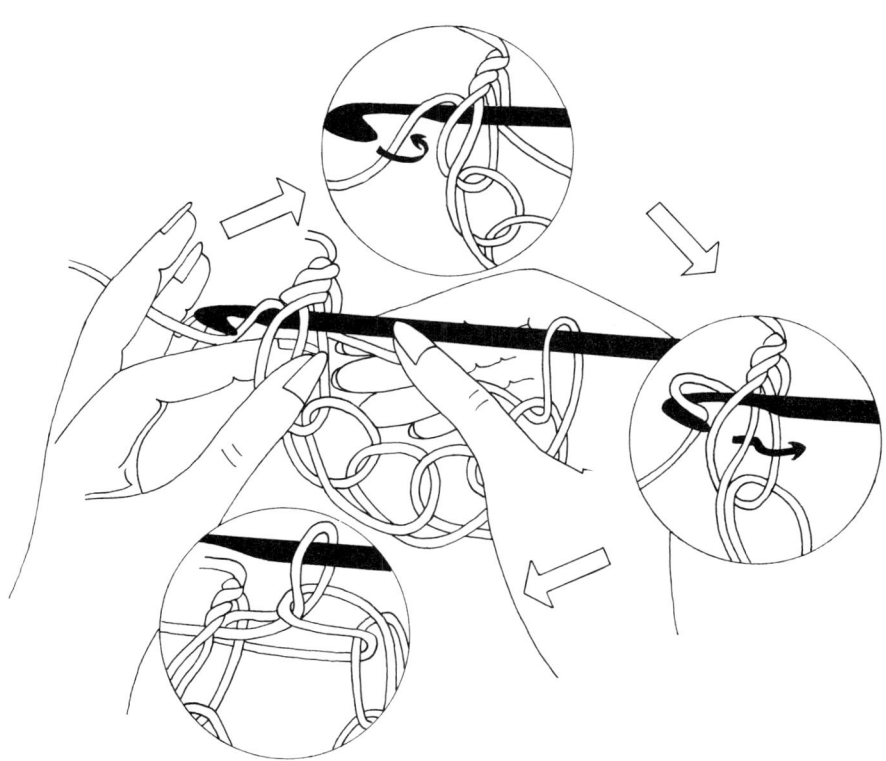

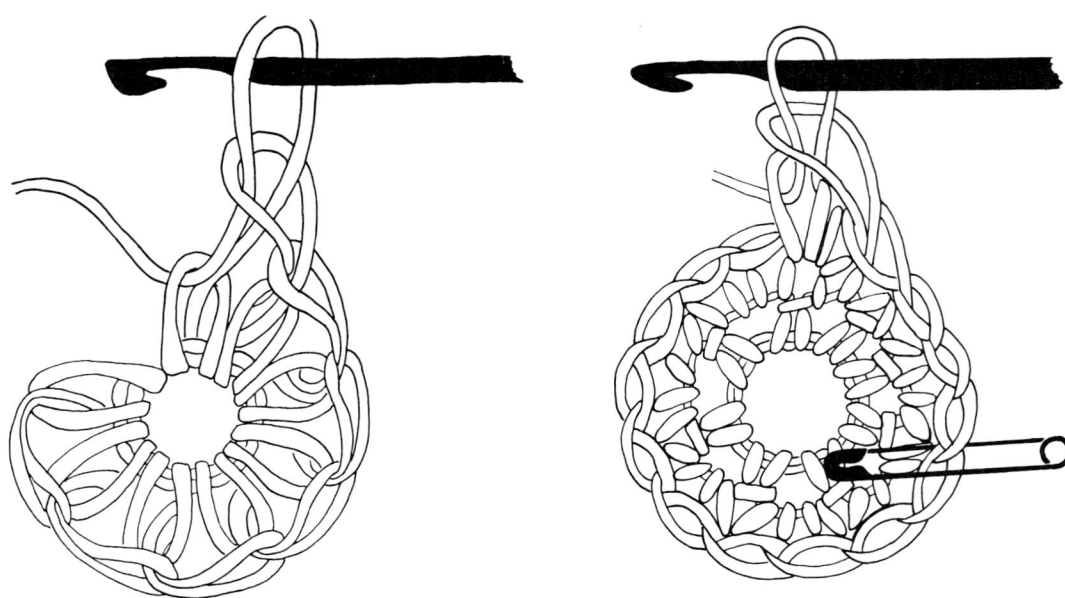

Rounds of double crochet

The
Projects

2. V-Neck Pullover

Size
To fit chest size 96.5cm–102cm (38in–40in).

Materials
8 x 50g balls Loweth Shetland DK wool
3.50 and 4.00 crochet hooks

Tension
Dc is always worked in 2 lps unless otherwise stated.

Back

Rib

With 3.50 hook make 85 ch.
Row 1 Right side of work, 1 dc in 2nd ch from hook, 1 dc in each ch st (84 dc).
Row 2 1 ch, 1 dc in front lp of each dc to end of row. Rep last row until work measures 5cm (2in), 10 rows.
　With 4.00 hook work through 2 lps.
Row 1 1 ch, 1 dc in each dc to end of row.
　Rep last row until work measures 42cm (16½in).

Shape armhole

Row 1 Ss over 8 sts, 1 ch, 1 dc in each dc to last 8 sts. Turn.
Row 2 1 ch, 1 dc in each dc.
Row 3 1 ch (miss 1 dc, 1 dc in next dc) 1 dc in each dc to last 2 sts (miss 1 dc, 1 dc in next dc).
Rep last 2 rows until 60 sts rem **.
Rep Row 2 until work measures 61cm (24in). Fasten off.

Front

Work as for Back as far as **.

Right front

Next row, 1 ch, 1 dc in each dc, 30 times. Leave rem 30 sts. Turn.
Dec 1 st at beg and end of alt rows at armhole, 3 times.
Dec at neck every 3rd row until 20 dc rem, cont straight until work measures as Back.

Left front

Work as Right front, reverse shaping.

Borders

Neck

Right side of work, join at back.
Rnd 1 1 ch, dc evenly rnd neck, ss to 1 ch.
Rnd 2 1 ch, dc in the back st of each dc. Miss 1 dc each side of neck.
　Rep last rnd twice more. Fasten off.

Sleeves

Rnd 1 Join with 1 ch, 1 dc evenly rnd armhole.
Rnd 2 1 ch, 1 dc in the back of each dc, ss to 1 ch.
　Rep last rnd twice more.

3. Waistcoat

Size

To fit chest size 86cm–97cm (34in–38in).
Length from shoulder 66cm (26in).

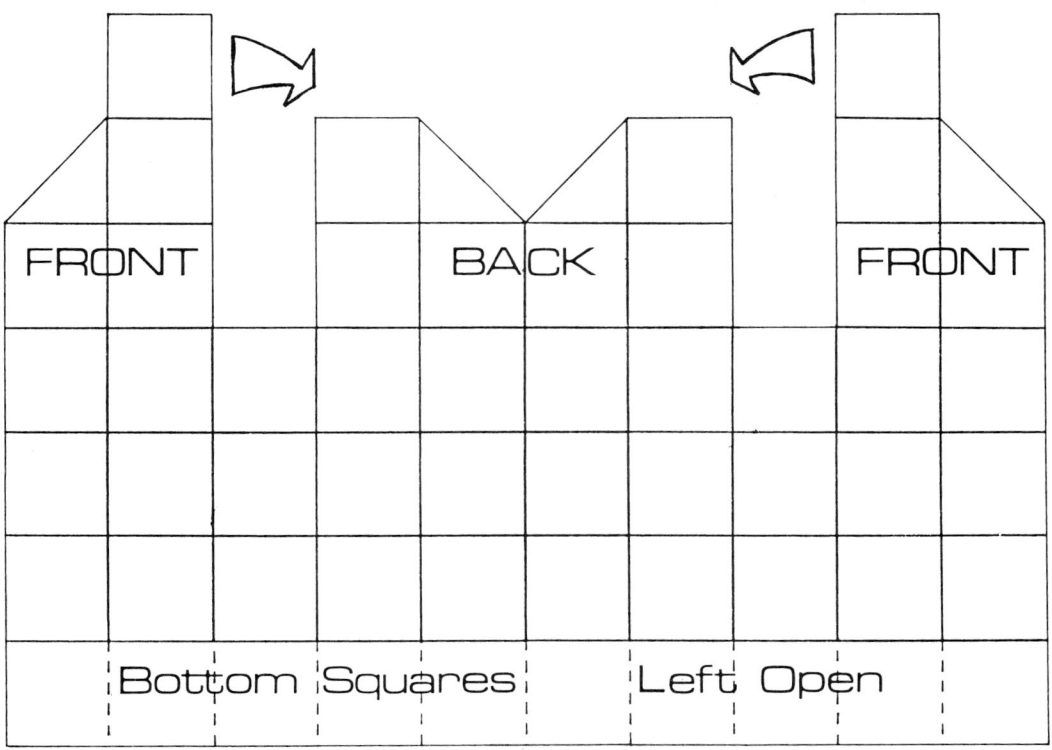

Materials

8 x 50g balls Emu Supermatch DK wool
    1 airforce blue
    2 light blue
    2 beige
    3 light brown
4.00 crochet hook
Make 54 squares and 4 triangles

Method for square or triangle

Square

Note To join colours, hook into sp, pull through thread, yoh and draw through.
With *Dark Blue* DK wool and a 4.00 hook, make 5 ch, join with a ss to form a ring.
Rnd 1 3 ch, 2 tr into ring. (3 ch, 3 tr) 3 times, 3 ch. Join with a ss to the

top of 1st 3 ch, pull thread through st (clip thread just enough to work over end on next rnd).

Rnd 2 *(light blue)* (2 ch, 2 tr, 2 ch, 3 tr) all into same sp. * (2 ch, 3 tr, 2 ch, 3 tr) all into next sp. Rep from * twice more.

2 ch, join with a ss to top of 1st 2 ch. Fasten off.

Rnd 3 *(beige)* Starting in 2 ch sp, one side of square, 2 ch, 2 tr, 2 ch, (3 tr, 2 ch, 3 tr) into corner sp. *(2 ch, 3 tr, 2 ch, side) (3 tr, 2 ch, 3 tr) into corner sp. Rep from * twice more. 2 ch, join with a ss. Fasten off.

Rnd 4 *(light brown)* (note 2 ch to start which counts as 1 tr) Work in corners (3 tr, 2 ch, 3 tr) only. 2 ch between groups of 3 tr. 1 group of 3 tr in side sps.

This completes one square for waistcoat.

If a larger square for making a bag, cushion, shawl or bedspread is required just continue to work in corners (3 tr, 2 ch, 3 tr).

Square measures 10cm (4in).

Triangle

Note To join colours, hook into sp, pull through thread, yoh and draw through.

With *Dark Blue* DK wool and a 4.00 hook make 5 ch, join with a ss to 1st ch to form a ring.

Rnd 1 3 ch, 2 tr into ring. (3 ch, 3 tr) 3 times. 3 ch, join with a ss to top of 1st 3 ch. Fasten off.

Rnd 2 *(light blue)* (2 ch, 2 tr, 2 ch, 3 tr) into sp. *(2 ch, 3 tr, 2 ch, 3 tr) into next sp. Rep from * once more. Fasten off.

Rnd 3 *(beige)* Join at beg of light blue. 2 ch sp (2ch, 2 tr, 2 ch, 3 tr) into sp. *(2 ch, 3 tr) into next sp (side). (2 ch, 3 tr, 2 ch, 3 tr) into corner sp. Rep from * once more. Fasten off.

Rnd 4 *(light brown)* Join at beg of beige. 2 ch sp (2 ch, 2 tr, 2 ch, 3 tr) into sp. *(2 ch, 3 tr) into next sp. Rep from * once more (side). 2 ch, 3 tr, 2 ch, 3 tr into corner sp. *(2 ch, 3 tr into next sp). Rep from * once more, ending (2 ch, 3 tr, 2 ch, 3 tr) into next sp.

Do not break yarn. (2 ch. 1 dc into top of beige tr) 2 ch, 1 dc into top of blue tr) (2 ch, 1 dc into dark blue ch sp) continue across ending (2 ch, 1 dc into top of light brown, 3 ch. Fasten off.

Making up

Put squares together as shown in chart (figure 12).

How to join squares

Start with 2 squares tog, right sides inside.

Match each ch st and tr sts tog.

Join to 1 ch st at corners tog, leaving the other ch st side edge. *(Hook through front lp of tr st to back lp of tr st with a ss. Rep twice more, then ss into ch sts tog twice). Rep from * ending ss into corner st tog, do not break yarn.

Take 2 more squares, ss across as 1st 2 squares.

Continue this way until 10 squares across have been joined (20 squares). Follow chart working squares across, then ss squares sideways, leaving 10 squares bottom edge.

Border

Left bottom edge – right side, 1 dc into back of each dc st rnd squares, turn to right front side edge, dc to triangle, dc into ch sts, 1 dc into back of each dc st rnd neck to centre back. Draw 4 shell patts tog (hook into 2 ch sp, yoh and draw through) rep 3 times more yoh and draw through 5 lps. Continue to dc left front as right front. Fasten off.

Join light blue into fasten off st wrong side of work, make a puff st into same st. *(2 ch then 1 puff st into 3rd dc.) Rep from * left side, rnd neck, then right side. Fasten off.

Right side of work, join into dc st, 3 ch side of puff st. *(3 dc into 2 ch sp). Rep from * right side, rnd neck then left side.

4. Party Top

Size

Chest 86cm (34in). Length from shoulder 51cm (20in).

Materials

4 x 20g balls George Picaud Feu d'artifice (Lurex)
1 x 40g ball No.1 mohair
3.00 crochet hook

Tension

5cm (2in) length. Note when to turn.

Yoke

With 3.00 hook and Lurex make 202 ch. Ss to 1st ch to form a circle. 2 ch.
Rnd 1 1 tr in each ch st (201 tr), ss to top of 2 ch. Turn.
Right side of work.
Rnd 2 *(8 ch, ss in next tr) rep from * 202 lps. Ss to 1st ch sp. Fasten off.
Rnd 3 Join mohair in 1st ch sp, 2 ch *(2 dc in each sp). Rep from *. Ss
to 1st dc. Fasten off.
Rnd 4 Join Lurex, right side of work. 2 ch, 1 tr into back of each dc to end
of rnd. Ss to top of 2 ch. Turn.
Rnd 5 As Rnd 2 (404 lps).
Rnd 6 Join mohair. 1 ch, 1 dc in each lp (202 dc). Fasten off.

Back

Row 1 Join Lurex, right side, in tr, 2 ch (1 tr into back of each dc) 60
times.
Row 2 (8 ch, ss in next tr). Rep from * to end of row (59 lps). Fasten off.

Front (arm, 141 dc each side; front, 6l dc)

Row 1 Leave 141 dc. Join to next tr, 2 ch, 1 tr in each tr (60 times).
Row 2 (8 ch, ss in next tr) rep from * to end of row (59 lps). Fasten off.

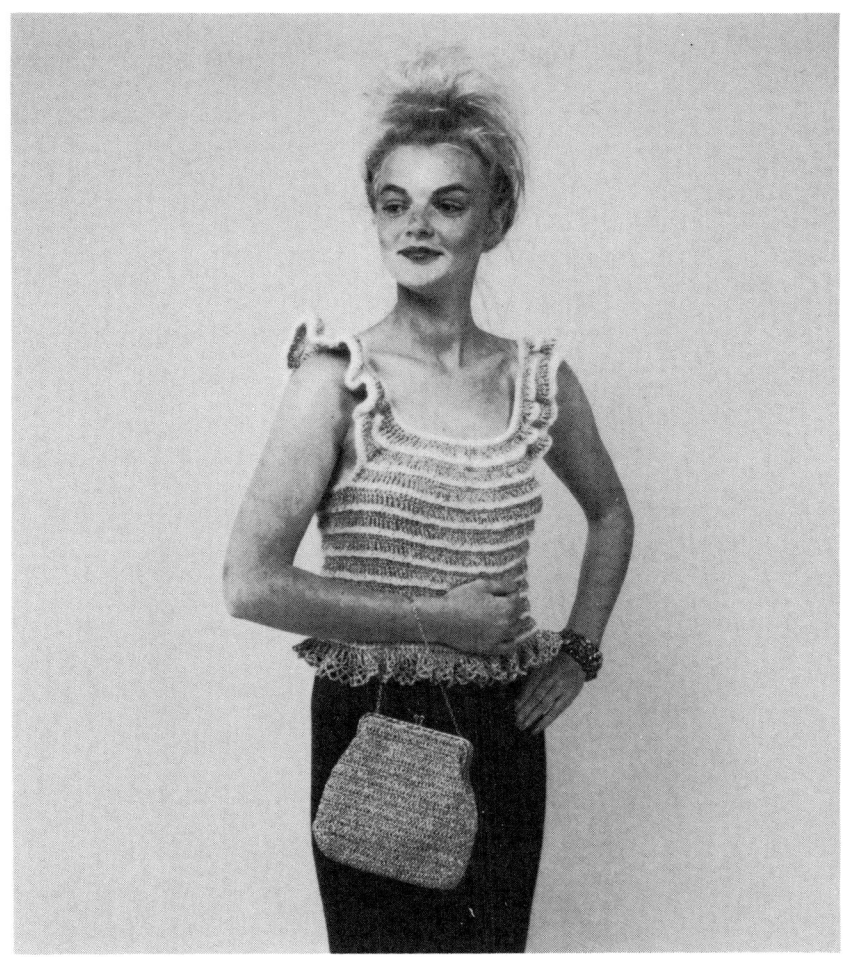

Party top and evening bag

Back

Rnd 1 Join mohair, wrong side, 1 ch, 1 dc in each lp, 59 times, then continue to make 12 ch. Arm, front, continue 1 dc in each lp make 12 ch. Ss to 1st ch. Fasten off. Turn.

Rnd 2 Join Lurex, 2 ch in fasten off st. 1 tr in each ch, 11 times. 1 tr in back of dc st, 59 times. 1 tr in each ch. 1 tr in back of each dc st, 59 times. Ss to top of 2 ch. Turn.

Rnd 3 Wrong side. *(8 ch, ss in next tr.) Rep from *. Ss to beg of 1st lp (142 lps).

Rnd 4 Join mohair in lp, 1 ch, 1 dc in each lp (142 dc). Ss to 1st dc. Fasten off.

Rnd 5 Right side. Join Lurex, 3 ch, 1 tr in back of each dc st. Ss to top of 3 ch (142 tr).

Last 3 rows form patt. Rep patt 9 times from the neck.

Wrong side. After Rnd 3: ss to top of next lp. *(3 ch, ss, turn to next lp. Rep from * to end of rnd, ending ss in 1st ss.

Right side * (3 ch, ss in next ss) rep from * to end of rnd.

Next rnd * (5 ch, ss in centre of 3 ch) rep from * to end of rnd.

Next rnd * (6 ch, ss in centre of 5 ch) rep from * to end of rnd.

Borders

Join mohair underarm, 12 dc across ch st edge. 5 dc in Lurex edge, 1 dc in each back st of mohair, dc rnd to 5 dc in Lurex edge. Ss to 1st dc. Fasten off.

Neck

Wrong side. Join 1 ch, 1 dc between each tr st to 1st ch st. Ss to join. Fasten off.

5. Evening Bag

Size

19cm (7½in) length, 20cm (8in) across, 1st row of tr.
Handle 14cm (5½in)
Lining 38cm (15in) length, 46cm (18in) across

Materials

1 x 20g ball George Picaud Feu d'artifice (Lurex)
3.00 crochet hook

Tension

6 rows tr. Length 5cm (2in). 12 trs across 5 cm (2in).

With 3.00 crochet hook, make 35 ch
Row 1 Miss 1 ch, 1 dc in each ch st (34 dc).
Row 2 1 ch, 1 dc in each dc.
Rep Row 2 for 10 more rows. Do not turn.
Rnd 1 10 dc, side edge, turn to ch st edge. 1 dc in each ch st (34 dc).
10 dc in side edge (54 dc rnd). Ss to top of 2 ch. Turn.
Rnd 2 2 ch, 1 tr in each dc to end of rnd. Ss to top of 2 ch.
Rnd 3 2 ch, 1 tr in each tr, to end of rnd. Ss to top of 2 ch.
Rep last rnd, until 19 tr rnds have been worked from beg. Fasten off.
   Sew in lining, then sew edge of Lurex to handle.

6. Jumper

Size

To fit chest 96cm–101cm (38in-40in)

Length from shoulder

58cm (23in)

Sleeve seam

41cm (16in).

Materials

9 x 50g balls, Emu Supermatch DK wool
4.00 and 3.50 crochet hooks

Cross treble

Tension

4 rows – 5cm (2in).
With 4.00 crochet hook, make 21 ch.
Row 1 1 tr in 3rd ch from hook, 1 tr into each ch st to end of row (19 tr),
2 ch.
Row 2 Miss 1st tr, 1 tr into next tr, 1 tr fr of last tr called (cross treble –
cr tr). *(1 cr tr into next 2 tr). Rep from * to end of row, ending 1 tr into
last tr, 2 ch.
Row 3 1 tr into 1st tr, 1 tr into each tr.
   Last 2 rows form patt.

Back and front alike

With 4.00 crochet hook make 93 ch.
Row 1 Right side of work. 1 tr into 3rd ch from hook, 1 tr into each ch st
to end of row (91 tr) 2 ch.
Row 2 Miss 1st tr, 1 tr into next tr. 1 tr fr of last tr. * (1 cr tr into next 2
tr.) Rep from * to end of row, ending 1 tr into last tr, 2 ch.
Row 3 1 tr into 1st tr, 1 tr into each tr.
   Last 2 rows form patt.
   Rep last 2 rows until work measures 51cm (20in) ending tr row.
   Fasten off.

Sleeves

With 4.00 crochet hook make 55 ch.
Row 1 1 tr into 3rd ch from hook, 1 tr into each ch st to end of row (53
tr), 2 ch.
Row 2 Miss 1st tr. *(1 cr tr into next 2 tr.) Rep from * to end of row.
Ending 1 tr into last tr, 2 ch.
Row 3 1 tr into 1st tr, 1 tr into each tr.
Rep last 2 rows until work measures 32cm (12½in). Fasten off (top of
sleeve).

Making up

Sew shoulders tog (9 cr tr patts across) 13cm (5in).
Sew side seams 33cm (13in) from bottom edge.
Fold sleeve in half, centre st to shoulder seam, place the cast off edge
evenly into armhole, then sew in side seams of sleeve.

Border

Join at bottom edge of jumper with 3.50 crochet hook.
Rnd 1 Make 1 ch into ch st. *(1 dc into each ch st (3 times) miss 1 ch st.)
Rep from * to end of rnd, ss to 1st ch st, 2 ch, turn.
Rnd 2 1 tr into each dc, to end of rnd. Ss into top of 2 ch, 1 ch, turn.
Rnd 3 1 dc into each tr, to end of rnd. Ss into 1 ch turn. Rep last 2 rnds
6 times. Fasten off.

Sleeve

Border as bottom edge.
Rnds 2 and 3 to be rep 5 times.

Neck

Picot edge
Join right side with 3.50 hook at shoulder. *(3 ch, ss into 1st ch from
hook, miss 1 tr st, ss into next tr.) Rep from * to beg of rnd. Fasten off.

7. Short Sleeve Alpaca Jumper

Size

To fit chest 86cm (34in). Length from neck 51cm (20in).

Materials

5 x 50g balls George Picaud Alpaca. 4.00 and 3.50 crochet hooks.

Shell stitch

Tension

4 rows 5cm (2in).

With 4.00 hook, make 30 ch.
Right side of work, 1 dc in 2nd ch from hook, 1 dc in each ch st then join to 1st dc, with a ss to form a ring.
Rnd 1 2 ch (counts as 1 tr) *(miss 2 dc 5 tr in next dc, miss 2 dc 1 tr in next dc). Rep from * to end of rnd.
Ss to top of 1 ch (5 shells). Turn.
Rnd 2 2 ch 4 tr in same sp *(1 tr in 3 tr centre of shell, miss 2 tr 5 tr in next 1 tr). Rep from * to end of rnd.
Ss to top of 2 ch. Turn.
Rnd 3 Ss in the 1 tr 2 ch. 4 tr in same sp *(1 tr in 3rd tr centre of shell, miss 2 tr, 5 tr, in next 1 tr). Rep from * to end of rnd. Ss to top of 2 ch. Turn.
Rep last rnd which forms patt.

Tension

4 rows 5cm (2in) square 2 patts across.

With 4.00 hook make 187 ch.
Row 1 Right side of work, 1 dc in 2nd ch from hook, 1 dc in each ch st then join to 1st dc, with a ss to form a ring.
Rnd 1 2 ch (counts as 1 tr). *(Miss 2 dc, 5 tr in next dc, miss 2 dc, 1 tr in next dc). Rep from * to end of rnd. Ss to top of 2 ch, turn (31 shells).
Rnd 2 2 ch, 4 tr in same sp. *(1 tr in 3rd tr, centre of shell, miss 2 tr, 5 tr in next 1 tr). Rep from * to end of rnd, ss to top of 2 ch, turn.
Rnd 3 Ss in the 1 tr, 2 ch 4 tr in same sp. *(1 tr in 3rd tr, centre of shell miss tr, 5 tr in next 1 tr). Rep from * to end of rnd. Ss to top of 2 ch, turn.
   Rep last rnd until 32 rnds have been worked from beg to armholes.
   Divide front and back.

Front

Row 1 Ss in the 1 tr, 2 ch, 4 tr in same sp. *(1 tr in 3rd tr, centre of shell, miss 2 tr, 5 tr in next 1 tr). Rep from * 14 times. 1 tr in 3rd tr, centre of shell, turn.
Row 2 2 ch, 4 tr in same tr, *(1 tr in 3rd tr. Centre of shell, miss 2 tr, 5 tr in next 1 tr). Rep from * to last shell, 1 tr in centre of shell, turn.
   Rep last row 14 times more (16 patts length from armhole). Fasten off.

Back

Row 1 Miss 5 tr, join to centre of shell, 2 ch, 1 tr in same sp. *(Miss 2 tr, 5 tr, in next 1 tr, 1 tr in 3rd tr, centre of shell). Rep from * ending 5 tr in 1 tr, leaving 5 tr (1 shell), turn.
Row 2 Ss into 3rd tr, 2 ch, 1 tr in same sp. *(miss 2 tr, 5 tr in next 1 tr, 1 tr in 3rd tr, centre of shell.) Rep from * ending 5 tr in 1 tr.
   Rep last row until there are 16 patts length from arm. Fasten off.

Sleeves

Make 73 ch.
Row 1 1 dc in 2nd ch from hook, 1 dc in each ch st.
Row 2 2 ch *(miss 2 dc, 5 tr in next dc, miss 2 dc, 1 tr in next dc). Rep from * to end of row (12 shells).
Row 3 2 ch, 4 tr in same tr. *(1 tr in 3rd tr, centre of shell, miss 2 tr, 5 tr, in next 1 tr.) Rep from * to last 6 tr, 1 tr in 3rd tr, centre of shell, miss 2 tr, 5 tr in 1 tr.
Row 4 Ss into 3rd tr, 2 ch, 1 tr in same sp. *(Miss 2 tr, 5 tr in 1 tr, 1 tr in 3rd tr centre of shell.) Rep from * to end of row.
   Rep 3rd and 4th rows, until 17 shells have been worked from beg. Fasten off.

Making up

Wrong side, sew shoulders tog, 3 shells across, then sew in sleeves.

Borders

Neck

Wrong side, join at shoulder *(1 dc in each tr of shell, twice. (Centre tr, 1 dc, 2 ch, ss in same tr). 1 dc in each tr, twice, ss in the next 1 tr). Rep from * to beg of 1st dc, ss to join. Fasten off.

Sleeves

Right side, 1 dc in each ch st, to beg. Ss to 1st dc.
Rnd 1 1 dc in each dc to end of rnd.
   Rep last rnd twice more.

Bottom edge

Work as sleeve.

8. Ribbed Cotton Boob Tube

Size

To fit bust 86cm (34in). Length 28cm (11in).

Materials

George Picaud quality cotton Cannelle, 2 balls cream, 2 green
No. 3 crochet hook

Ribbed pattern

Note

2 ch counts as 1 tr. Sample measures length 6cm (2½in).

Materials

With 4.00 crochet hook and DK yarn. Make 20 ch.
Row 1 1 tr into 3rd ch from hook, 1 tr into each ch st to end of row (18 tr).
Row 2 2 ch (1 tr fr of next tr) (1 tr bk of next tr) called (1 tr fr, 1 tr bk). Rep 1 tr fr, 1 tr bk to end of row, ending 1 tr bk of 2 ch.
Row 3 2 ch (1 tr bk, tr fr). Rep to end of row, ending 1 tr fr of 2 ch.
  Rep Rows 2 and 3 twice more. Fasten off.

Tension

4cm (1½in) length of 1 patt.

With 3.00 crochet hook, and cream yarn, make 63 ch.
Row 1 Right side, 1 tr in 3rd ch from hook, 1 tr in each ch st to end of row, do not break off cotton.
Row 2 Join green, 2 ch, 1 tr fr of each tr to end of row, ending 1 tr fr of 2 ch.
Row 3 2 ch, 1 tr in each tr, ending 1 tr in top of 2 ch.
Row 4 Cream, 2 ch, 1 tr fr of each tr, to end of row ending 1 tr fr of 2 ch.
Row 5 2 ch, 1 tr in each tr, ending 1 tr in top of 2 ch.
  Last 4 rows form patt. Rep patt 21 times. Then work Rows 2 and 3. Break off green. Work Row 4 cream.

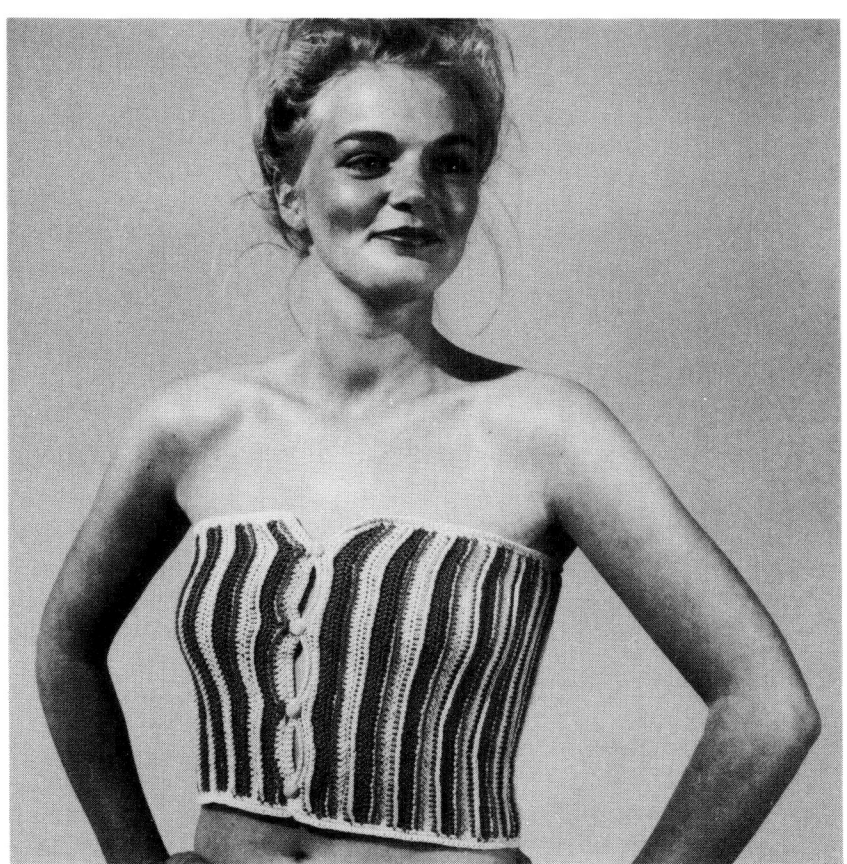

Left side

Next row, 1 dc in each tr, to end of row. (This edge to sew on buttons.) Turn to bottom edge, 4 dc in each panel.

Right side

1 dc in each ch st to top, then 4 dc in each panel rnd top edge to left side corner, turn.

Top edge

1 ch, 1 dc in each dc, turn.

Right side

Buttonholes. Ss in each dc, 3 times. *(3 ch, miss 2 dc. Ss in each dc, 14 times). Rep from * 3 times more. Ss in next 8 dc.

Bottom edge

1 dc in each dc to left side, 1 dc in each dc to top. Ss in corner st. Fasten off.

9. Family Ribbed Sweater

Size

To fit bust

81 (86 91 96) cm 32 (34 36 38) in

length from Shoulder

48 (53 58 63) cm 19 (21 23 25) in

Sleeve seam

38 (43 46 48) cm 15 (17 18 19) in

Materials

14 (16 18 20) 50g balls of Chanteleine Myriam DK wool
4.00 crochet hook

Tension

Length – 6 rows = 5cm (2in).
See page 00 for instructions for how to work rib.

Back

With 4.00 crochet hook, make 76 (82 88 94) ch.
Row 1 Miss 2 ch, 1 tr into 3rd ch from hook, 1 tr into each ch to end of row.
Row 2 Wrong side, 2 ch *(1 tr fr, 1 tr bk). Rep from * 36 (39 42 45) times. 1 tr fr, 1 tr bk of 2 ch.
Row 3 2 ch * (1 tr bk, 1 tr fr). Rep from * 36 (39 42 45) times. 1 tr bk, 1 tr fr of 2 ch.
   Last 2 rows form patt.
   Rep last 2 rows until work measures 52 (56, 60, 64) cm (20½ (22, 23½, 25) in ending on wrong side of work. Fasten off.

Front

Work as back until work measures 41 (43, 46, 48) cm (16 (17, 18, 19) in ending on wrong side of work.

Shape neck

Right front

Row 1 2 ch * (1 tr bk, 1 tr fr). Rep from * 8 (10, 10, 12) times, 1 tr bk. Turn.
Row 2 2 ch *(1 tr bk, 1 tr fr). Rep from * 8 (10, 10, 12) times, 1 tr bk of 2 ch.
   Rep last 2 rows 4 times more. Fasten off.

Left front

Leave 34 (34, 36, 36) sts neck, join to bk of next tr.
Work to match Right Front.

Sleeves

Make 68 (72, 76, 80) ch.
   Work patt as back until work measures 38 (41, 43, 38) cm. (15 (16, 17, 15).
   Fasten off.

Making up

Fold sleeve in half. Join centre st at the top of sleeve to top of shoulder seam. Sew in sleeve.

Borders

Neck

Join at corner left shoulder. 1 ch, dc rnd neck. Ss to 1st 1 ch, 1 ch.
Rnd 1 1 dc into each dc (dec 1st into each corner).
Rnd 2 1 dc into each dc.
Rep last 2 rnds twice more. Fasten off.

Cuff

Join at sleeve seam with 1 ch *(1 dc, miss 1 st). Rep from * to end of rnd. Ss to 1st 1 ch. Then work 12 rnds dc. Fasten off.

Bottom edge

Work 13 rnds, dc into each dc. Fasten off.
   Rows can be adjusted for length required.

10. Ribbed Hat

Size

Average

Materials

2 x 50g balls Chanteleine Myriam DK wool
4.00 crochet hook

Tension

As ribbed sweater page 32.

Note 2 ch counts as 1 tr.
Make 5 ch, ss to 1st ch st.
Rnd 1 2 ch, 15 tr into centre. Ss to top of 2 ch (16 tr includes 2 ch).
Rnd 2 2 ch, 2 tr into each tr. Ss to top of 2 ch (32 tr).
Rnd 3 2 ch *(2 tr into next tr, 1 tr into next tr). Rep from * ending 2 tr into next tr. Ss to top of 2 ch (48 tr).
Rnd 4 2 ch *(2 tr into next tr, 1 tr into next tr, twice). Rep from *. Ss to top of 2 ch (64 tr).
Rnd 5 2 ch *(2 tr into next tr, 1 tr into each tr, 3 times). Rep from * ending 1 tr into each tr, twice. Ss to top of 2 ch (80 tr).
Rnd 6 2 ch *(2 tr into next tr, 1 tr into each tr, 9 times). Rep from * ending 1 tr into each tr, 8 times. Ss to top of 2 ch (88 tr).

Right side of hat

Rnd 7 2 ch *(1 tr fr of each tr). Rep from * 87 times. Ss to top of 2 ch.
Rnd 8 2 ch *(1 tr fr, 1 tr bk). Rep from * to end of rnd, ending 1 tr fr. Ss to top of 2 ch. Turn.
Rnd 9 2 ch *(1 tr bk, 1 tr fr). Rep from * to end of rnd, ending 1 tr bk. Ss to top of 2 ch. Turn.
Rep last 2 rnds 6 times more. Turn.

Turning of hat

Next rnd 2 ch, 1 tr fr into each tr. Ss to top of 2 ch. Turn.
Next rnd Ss to next st, 2 ch *(1 tr fr, 1 tr bk). Rep from * to end of rnd, ending 1 tr fr of 2 ch. Ss to top of 2 ch. Turn.
Last rnd 2 ch *(1 tr bk, 1 tr fr). Rep from * to end of rnd, ending 1 tr bk. Ss to top of 2 ch. Fasten off.

11. Scarf

Length

Without fringe 150cm (95in)

Materials

5 x 50g balls Chanteleine Myriam DK wool
4.00 crochet hook

Tension

As ribbed sweater page 32.

With 4.00 hook make 42 ch.
Row 1 Miss 2 ch, tr into 3rd ch from hook, 1 tr into each ch to end of row.
Row 2 2 ch *(1 tr fr, 1 tr bk). Rep from * ending 1 tr fr, 1 tr bk of 2 ch.
Row 3 2 ch *(1 tr bk, 1 tr fr). Rep from * ending 1 tr bk, 1 tr fr of 2 ch.
   Last 2 rows form patt.
   Rep last 2 rows until work measures 146cm (57½in).
   Next row, 2 ch *(miss 1 dc, 1 tr into next dc, 1 ch). Rep from * to end of row, ending 1 tr into last dc (19 sps for fringe).
   Fasten off.
   Join at bottom end of scarf. 1 ch *(1 dc into each ch st). Rep from * to end of row (19 sps for fringe). Fasten off.

How to fringe

Cut required lengths of yarn and fold in half. Place crochet hook into sp. Place folded ends over hook, and pull through sp. Then pull the cut ends firmly through the loop.

Fringe for the scarf

Into the spaces insert 4 strands 25cm (10in) each length.

12. Necklace

Size

Average. Length can be adjusted, less or extra ch each side.

Materials

1 x 20g ball George Picaud Lurex
2.50 and 1.75 crochet hooks
15 shank buttons
Small piece of Velcro for fastener

With 2.50 crochet hook, make 91 ch.
Row 1 1 dc in 2nd ch from hook, 1 dc in each ch st (90 dc).
Row 2 With 2.50 hook, 10 dc. *(Button facing, 1.75 hook, place into shank, yoh, pull stitch on hook through firmly. 2.50 hook, 5 dc). Rep from * until 15 buttons have been placed, ending 10 dc.
   Work Row 1 twice. Fasten off.
Place Velcro at each end to fasten.

13. Bracelet

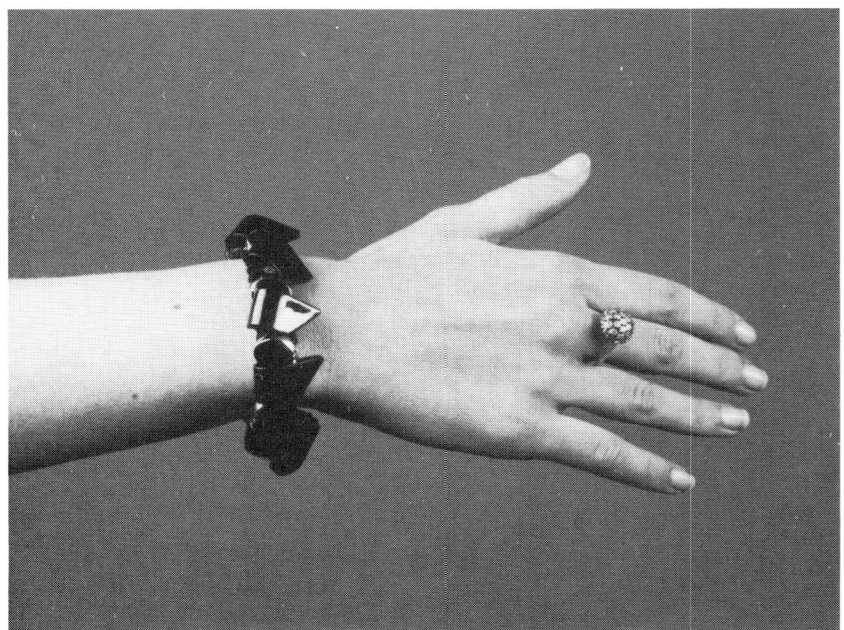

Size

Average. Can be adjusted, less or extra ch and buttons.

Materials

1 spool black shirring elastic (20m)
2.50 and 1.75 crochet hooks
10 large shank buttons
10 buttons in a contrasting colour

With 2.50 crochet hook, make 40 ch. Ss to 1st ch st to form a ring.
Rnd 1 1 ch, 1 dc in each ch st. Ss to 1 ch. Turn.
Rnd 2 1 ch, 2 dc. * (Button facing, 1.75 hook, place into shank, yoh, pull stitch on hook through firmly. 2.50 hook, 2 dc, change to contrast button, work the same as 1st button, 2 dc). Rep from * to end of rnd. Ss to 1st dc. Turn.
  Work Rnd 1 twice. Fasten off.

14. Wedding Dress

Size

To fit bust 86cm (34in).

Materials

21 x 25g balls Shetland lace   2.50 crochet hook.
1 spool gold elastic

Puff st

Raise lp, yoh, draw through, yoh and draw through, yoh and draw through 5 lps. *(2 ch, miss 1 tr. Next puff st, yoh, hook through 2nd tr and draw through, yoh and draw through, yoh and draw through 5 lps). Rep from * to form patt.

Yoke

With 2.50 crochet hook make 150 ch. Ss to 1st ch st, turn.

Rnd 1 2 ch, 1 tr in same sp. *(Miss 1 dc, 2 tr in next dc.) Rep from * to end of rnd. Ss to top of 2 ch, turn.

Rnd 2 Work puff st in every 2nd tr to end of rnd. Ss to top of 1st puff st, turn.

Rnd 3 Ss into sp, 2 ch, 2 tr *(3 tr in each sp). Rep from * to end of rnd. Ss to top of 2 ch turn.

Rnd 4 *(3 ch, 1 dc in sp). Rep from * to end of rnd. Dc into beg of 3 ch. Turn.

Rnd 5 3 ch, ss into next dc (4 ch, ss in same dc called 1 picot). *(3 ch, ss into next dc. 4 ch, ss in same dc) rep from * to end of rnd, ending 1 picot in last dc. Turn.

Rnd 6 Ss in 3 ch sp. *(6 ch ss to next sp) rep from * to end of rnd, turn.

Rnd 7 Ss in centre of 6 ch sp. *(5 ch, ss to next sp). Rep from * to end of rnd. Ss to 1st ch, turn.

Rnd 8 As Rnd 7, turn.

Rnd 9 1 ss to sp, 2 ch, 4 tr in sp *(5 tr in next sp). Rep from * to end of rnd, ss to top of 2 ch, turn.

Rnd 10 3 ch *(5 tr in centre of 5 tr, 1 tr between sp). Rep from * to end of rnd. Ss to top of 3 ch, turn.

Rnd 11 3 ch * (5 tr in centre tr of shell, 1 tr in 1 tr). Rep from * to end of rnd. Ss to top of 3 ch, turn.

Rep Rnd 11 until 12 more rnds have been worked.

Shape underarm

Front

Work patt across. *(20 shells ending 1 tr in 1 tr, make 17 ch. Miss 17 shells for sleeve. Join to back with 1 tr.) Rep from * to beg of rnd. Ss to top of 3 ch, turn.

Rnd 1 *(3 ch, 5 tr in 3rd ch) rep from * twice more across ch sts (underarm). 1 tr in 1 tr, work across 20 shell patts ending 1 tr in 1 tr). Rep from * once more to beg, ending ss to top of 3 ch, turn.

Rnd 2 3 ch *(5 tr in centre of shell, 1 tr in 1 tr). Rep from * to ending of rnd. Ss to top of 3 ch, turn.

Rep Rnd 2 18 times more.

Waist

Rnd 1 Join elastic with wool working 2 tog, 1 tr in 1 tr. Turn.

Rnd 2 *(1 tr in each 1 tr, 5 times, miss 1 tr.) Rep from * to end of rnd, turn.

Rnds 3 and 4 As Rnd 1

Rnd 5 As Rnd 2, ending 2 tr, ss to top of 2 ch, turn.

Rnds 6, 7 and 8 As Rnd 1

Rnd 9 3 ch, 1 tr in each 1 tr, 4 times. *(2 tr in next tr, 1 tr in each 1 tr, 5 times.) Rep from * to end of rnd. Ss to top of 3 ch, turn.

Rnds 10 and 11 As Rnd 1

Rnd 12 As Rnd 9

Rnd 13 As Rnd 1

Rnd 14 3 ch *(5 tr in 3rd tr, 1 tr in 3rd tr.) Rep from * ending 5 tr in 3rd tr, ss to top of 3 ch, turn.

Rep last rnd 4 times more.

Rnd 19 3 ch, 1 tr in same st. Miss 1 tr *(5 tr in centre of shell, 2 tr in 1 tr). Rep from * to end of rnd. Ss to top of 3 ch, turn.

Rep last rnd 4 times more.

Rnd 24 3 ch *(5 tr in centre of shell) (1 tr in 1st of 2 tr in sp of 2 tr, 1 tr). Rep from * to beg of rnd. Ss to top of 3 ch, turn.

Rnd 25 3 ch *(5 tr in centre of shell. 1 tr in each tr, 3 times). Rep from * to beg of rnd ending 1 tr, 1 tr in sp. Ss to top of 3 ch, turn.

Rnd 26 3 ch, 1 tr in 1 tr, twice. *(5 tr in centre of shell.) (1 tr in 1 tr, 3 times.) Rep from * ending 1 shell. Ss to top of 3 ch, turn.

Rnd 27 As Rnd 25, ending 1 tr in 1 tr twice. Ss to top of 3 ch, turn.

Rnd 28 As Rnd 26

Rnd 29 As Rnd 25, ending 1 tr in 1 tr twice. Ss to top of 3 ch, turn.

Rnd 30 3 ch, 1 tr in 1 tr, 2 tr in 1 tr, 1 tr in next 1 tr. *(5 tr in centre of shell, 1 tr in 1 tr, 2 tr in next 1 tr, 1 tr in 1 tr.) Rep from * ending 1 shell. Ss to top of 3 ch, turn.

Rnd 31 3 ch *(5 tr in centre of shell. 1 tr in 1 tr 4 times). Rep from * ending 1 tr in 1 tr, 3 times. Ss to top of 3 ch, turn.

Rnd 32 3 ch, 1 tr in 1 tr, 3 times *(5 tr in centre of shell. 1 tr in 1 tr 4 times). Rep from * ending 1 shell. Ss to top of 3 ch, turn.

Rep Rnds 31 and 32

Rnd 35 3 ch *(5 tr in centre of next shell) (work patt over 4 trs, 1 tr in 1 tr. 3 tr in centre sp of 4 trs. 1 tr in 1 tr). Rep from * ending 1 tr in 1 tr, 3 tr in centre sp. Ss to top of 3 ch, turn.

Rnd 36 *(3 tr in centre of 3 tr shell. 1 tr in 1 tr. 5 tr in centre of shell.) Rep from *. Ss to top of 3 ch, turn.

Rnd 37 *(5 tr in centre of shell. 1 tr in 1 tr. 3 tr in centre of 3 tr of shell.) Rep from *. Ss to top of 3 ch, turn.

Rep Rnds 36 and 37

Rnd 40 3 ch *(5 tr in centre of 3 tr of shell. 1 tr in 1 tr. 5 tr in centre of shell. 1 tr in 1 tr). Rep from * ending 5 tr in centre of shell. Ss to top of 3 ch, turn.

Rnd 41 3 ch *(5 tr in centre of shell. 1 tr in 1 tr). Rep from *. Ss to top of 3 ch, turn.

Rep Rnd 41 until work measures 135cm (53in) from shoulder, or required length. Do not make 3 ch on last rnd, turn.

Last rnd *(7 tr in centre of shell. Ss in 1 tr.(Rep from * ending with a ss. Fasten off.

Sleeves

Rnd 1 Join at underarm in the centre of shell, 3 ch, 4 tr in next tr. 5 tr in next shell. (1 tr in 1 tr twice, corner) then 1 shell. 1 tr in 1 tr. Ss to top of 3 ch, turn.

Rnd 2 3 ch * (5 tr in centre of shell, 1 tr in 1 tr). Rep from * to beg. Ss to top of 3 ch, turn.

Rep last rnd 32 times more.

Rnd 35 3 ch *(3 tr in centre of shell, 1 tr in 1 tr). Rep from * to beg. Ss to top of 3 ch, turn.

Rnd 36 As Rnd 35.

Rnd 37 3 ch * (2 tr in centre of shell, 1 tr in 1 tr). Rep from * to beg. Ss to top of 3 ch, turn.

Rnd 38 3 ch * (1 tr in 1 tr). Rep from * to beg. Ss to top of 3 ch, turn.

Rnds 39 and 40 As Rnd 38.

Rnd 41 3 ch, 2 tr in same sp. * (Miss 1 tr, 3 tr in next 1 tr.) Rep from * to beg. Ss to top of 3 ch, turn.

Rnd 42 3 ch *(3 tr in shell. 1 tr in sp). Rep from * to beg. Ss to top of 3 ch, turn.

Rnd 43 3 ch * (5 tr in centre of shell. 1 tr in 1 tr). Rep from * to beg. Ss to top of 3 ch, turn.

Rnd 44 As Rnd 43. Do not make 3 ch end of rnd, turn.

Last rnd * (7 tr in centre of shell. Ss in 1 tr.) Rep from * ending with a ss. Fasten off.

15. Bridesmaids' Dresses

Small size

To fit chest 61cm (24in). Length from shoulder 49cm (19in).

Materials

2 x 100g balls Chanteleine Catimini DK wool
4.50 and 5.00 crochet hooks
2 x 20mm knit pins

Tension

5 hlf tr patts square 5cm (2in). 2 Broomstick patts square 5cm (2in).

Broomstick skirt and sleeves

Tension

2 patts, length 5cm (2in).
Rnds Worked with 2.20mm knit pins and 5.00 hooks.
Lps are drawn through each dc st using 1 knit pin to take half the lps, then using 2nd pin for rem lps, turn. This forms a rnd without having a seam.
Rnd 1 With 5.00 hook, draw through lps in each dc st on to the knit pin.
Rnd 2 5 dc in 4 lps tog at beg of rnd *(4 dc in 4 lps tog). Rep from * to end of rnd. Ss to 1st dc, turn.
Rnd 3 Ss to next dc to keep patt even. Draw through lps in each dc to end of rnd.
Rnd 4 As Rnd 2.
  Last 2 rnds form patt.

With 4.50 hook make 124 ch. Ss to 1st ch st to form a ring.
Rnd 1 3 ch * (1 hlf tr in 2nd ch st, 1 ch). Rep from * to end of rnd. Ss into 1st hlf tr sp, turn.
Rnd 2 Right side. 3 ch *(1 hlf tr in hlf tr, 1 ch). Rep from * to end of rnd. Ss into 1st hlf tr sp, turn.
Rep Rnd 2 18 times more, do not break yarn.

Back

Row 1 3 ch (counts as hlf tr) * (1 hlf tr, 1 ch). Rep from * 24 times, turn.
Row 2 3 ch * (1 hlf tr, 1 ch), rep from * 23 times. 1 ch, 1 hlf tr in centre of 3 ch, turn.
Rep last row 5 times more, do not break yarn, continue to left shoulder.

Left shoulder

Row 1 3 ch * (1 hlf tr, 1 ch). Rep from * 5 times more, turn.
Row 2 3 ch * (1 hlf tr, 1 ch). Rep from * 4 times more, ending 1 hlf tr in centre of 3 ch, turn.
Rep last row 3 times more. Fasten off.

Right shoulder

Miss 11 hlf trs. Neck, join to next hlf tr, 3 ch * (1 hlf tr, 1 ch). Rep from *
4 times more to armhole, ending 1 hlf tr in centre of 3 ch.
Row 1 3 ch * (1 hlf tr, 1 ch) rep from * 4 times more, ending 1 hlf tr in
centre of 3 ch.
Rep last row 3 times more. Fasten off.

Front and shoulders

Match patt as back, miss 4 hlf trs each side for armholes, miss 11 hlf trs.
Neck, sew shoulders tog.

Skirt

Using 5.00 hook and 20mm pins. Join to right side back of waist with
hook * (2 dc in each ch st). Rep from * rnd waist to beg. Ss to 1st dc, turn.
Rnd 1 Draw through lps to end of rnd with two 20mm pins. Turn.
Rnd 2 5 dc in 1st 4 lps tog at beg of rnd. *(4 dc in 4 lps tog) rep from *
to end of rnd. Ss to 1st dc, turn.
Rnd 3 Ss to next dc to keep patt even. Draw through lps to end of rnd.
Rnd 4 As Rnd 2.
Last 2 rnds form patt. Rep patt 5 times from beg. Fasten off.

Sleeves

With 4.50 hook make 68 ch.
Row 1 Draw through lps in each ch st (68 lps).
Row 2 With 5.00 hook, 5 dc in 4 lps tog at beg of row * (4 dc in 4 lps tog).
Rep from * to end of row.
Row 3 Draw through lps in each dc.
Rep last 2 rows once more.
Row 6 5 dc in 8 lps tog, 4 dc in 8 lps tog, 3 times, 4 dc in 4 lps tog, then
4 dc in 8 lps tog, 4 times.
Row 7 Draw through lps in each dc.
Row 8 As Row 2. Fasten off.

Neck border

With 4.50 hook make 72 ch.
Row 1 Draw through lps in each ch st.
Row 2 5 dc in 4 lps tog at beg of row *(4 dc in 4 lps tog). Rep from * to
end of row. Ss to 1st dc to form a ring. Fasten off.
Sew tog bottom dc, place rnd neck with an overstitch for border to stand
up.
Sew in sleeves, fold in half placing 4 dc in 4 lps centre of sleeve, to
shoulder, the side seams.

Large size

To fit chest 71cm (28in). Length from shoulder 66cm (26in).

Materials

3 x 100g balls Chanteleine Catimini DK wool
4.50 and 5.00 crochet hooks
2 x 20mm knit pins

Tension

5 hlf tr patts square 5cm (2in).
2 Broomstick patts square 5cm (2in).

With 4.50 hook make 180 ch. Ss to 1st ch st to form a ring.
Rnd 1 3 ch * (1 hlf tr in 2nd ch st, 1 ch). Rep from * to end of rnd. Ss into 1st hlf tr sp, turn.
Rnd 2 Right side. 3 ch * (1 hlf tr in hlf tr, 1 ch). Rep from * to end of rnd. Ss into hlf tr sp, turn.
Rep Rnd 2 22 times more, do not break yarn.

Back

Row 1 3 ch (counts as hlf tr.) * (1 hlf tr, 1 ch). Rep from * 25 times, turn.
Row 2 3 ch * (1 hlf tr, 1 ch). Rep from * 24 times. 1 hlf tr in centre of 3 ch, turn.
Rep last row 6 times more, do not break yarn, continue to left shoulder.

Left shoulder

Row 1 3 ch * (1 hlf tr, 1 ch). Rep from * 5 times more, turn.
Row 2 3 ch * (1 hlf tr, 1 ch). Rep from * 4 times more, ending 1 hlf tr in centre of 3 ch, turn.
Rep last row 4 times more. Fasten off.

Right shoulder

Miss 12 hlf trs. Neck, join to next hlf tr, 3 ch * (1 hlf tr, 1 ch). Rep from * 4 times more to armhole, ending 1 hlf tr in centre of 3 ch.
Row 1 3 ch * (1 hlf tr, 1 ch) rep from * 4 times, ending 1 hlf tr in centre.
Rep last row 4 times more. Fasten off.

Front and shoulders

Match patt as back, miss 5 hlf trs each side for armholes. Miss 12 hlf trs. Neck, sew shoulders tog.

Skirt

Using 5.00 hook and 20mm pins.

Join to right side back of waist with hook *(2 dc in each ch st). Rep from * rnd waist to beg. Ss to 1st dc, turn.

Rnd 1 Draw through lps to end of rnd with two 20mm pins, turn.

Rnd 2 5 dc in 1st 4 lps tog at beg of rnd *(4 dc in 4 lps tog). Rep from * to end of rnd. Ss to 1st dc, turn.

Rnd 3 Ss to next dc to keep patt even. Draw through lps to end of rnd.

Rnd 4 As Rnd 2.

Last 2 rnds form patt. Rep patt 9 times from beg. Fasten off.

Sleeves

With 4.50 hook make 84 ch.

Row 1 Draw through lps in each ch st (84 lps).

Row 2 With 5.00 hook, 5 dc in 4 lps tog at beg of row *(4 dc in 4 lps tog.) Rep from * to end of row.

Row 3 Draw through lps in each dc.

Rep last 2 rows once more.

Row 6 5 dc in 8 lps tog, 4 dc in 8 lps tog, 4 times. 4 dc in 4 lps tog, then 4 dc in 8 lps tog, 5 times.

Row 7 Draw through lps in each dc.

Row 8 As Row 2. Fasten off.

Neck border

With 4.50 hook make 80 ch.

Row 1 Draw through lps in each ch st.

Row 2 5 dc in 4 lps tog at beg of row * (4 dc in 4 lps tog.) Rep from * to end of row. Ss to 1st dc to form a ring. Fasten off.

Sew tog bottom dc, place rnd neck with an overstitch for border to stand up.

Sew in sleeves, fold in half, placing 4 dc in 4 lps centre of sleeve, to shoulder, then side seams.

16. Cotton Bag

Size

Length 28cm (11in). Across bottom edge 41cm (16in).
Handle 21cm (8½in) across
Lining length 61cm (24in); across 89cm (35in)

Materials

4 x 50g balls George Picaud Coton à Tricoter
4.00 and 4.50 crochet hooks   15mm knit pin

Tension

4cm (1½in) across 2 patts.

Broomstick stitch

Tension

4cm (1½in) square

With 2 strands cotton tog and a 4.00 crochet hook, make 20 ch.
Row 1 With 1 15mm pin, draw lps through with hook in each ch st placing them on knit pin (20 lps).
Row 2 5.00 hook, 5 dc in 4 lps tog at beg of row. *(4 dc in 4 lps tog.) Rep from * to end of row (5 patts across).
Row 3 Draw through lps in each dc.
Row 4 As Row 2.
   Last 2 rows form patt.

Note Work 2 strands tog.

With 4.00 hook and 2 strands tog, make 80 ch.
Row 1 Draw through lps in each ch st (80 lps).
Row 2 With 5.00 hook, 5 dc in 4 lps tog at beg of row. * (4 dc in 4 lps tog.) Rep from * to end of row (20 patts across).
Row 3 Draw through lps in each dc.
Row 4 As Row 2.
Rep last 2 rows until 11 patts length have been worked from beg.

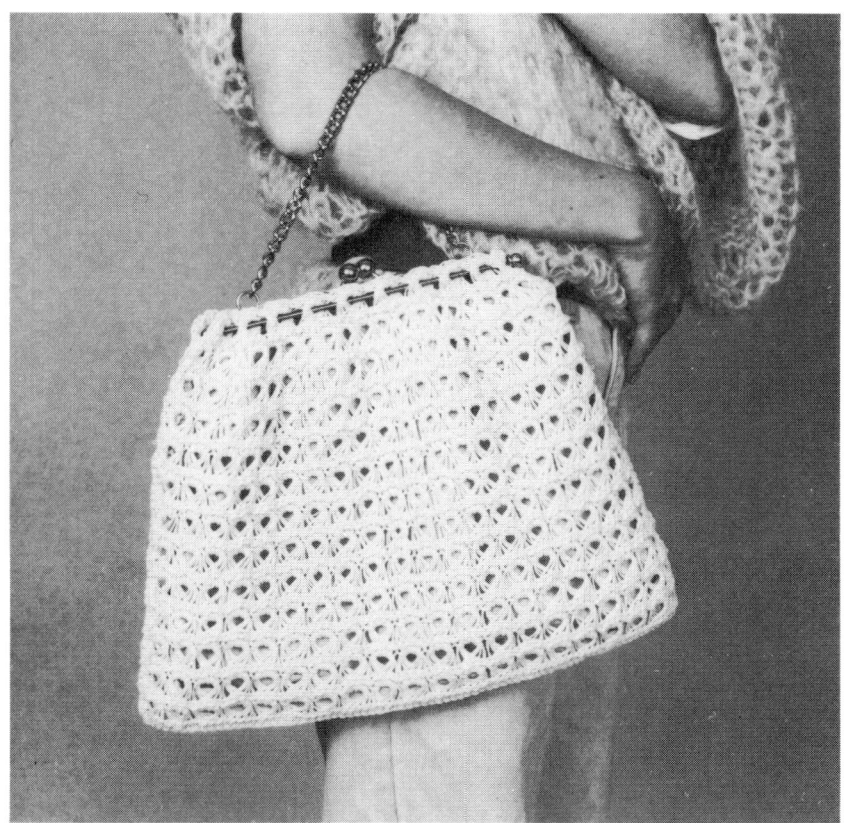

Shape top of bag

Row 1 Draw through lps in each dc.
Row 2 (4 dc in 4 lps tog) at beg of row. * (3 dc in 4 lps tog.) Rep from * to end of row.
Row 3 As Row 1.
Row 4 5 dc in 6 lps tog at beg of row. * (4 dc in 6 lps tog.) Rep from * to end of row. Fasten off.
Work another piece to match.
Open side edge of bag, 4 dc in each patt 4 times. Rep other 3 side edges in the same way.

Making up

Place 2 pieces tog match patt.
From the top of bag to the 5th patt at side edge. Join, hook through 2 patts tog, 4 dc in patts tog, to bottom edge. Continue to bottom edge, dc in ch sts tog then side edge, as other side.
Fasten off.
Fit in lining, leave top patt across, thread through handle.

17. Cushion Cover

Tunisian rug and cushion covers

Size

Cushion measures 41cm (16in) square – can easily be adjusted to size

Materials

4 x 40g balls Lister-Lee Machine-Washable Aran
1 blanket hook

Tension

4 sts: 3cm (1in)

Simple Tunisian stitch

Make 20 ch.

Row 1 Insert hook in the 2nd ch from hook, *(yrh, draw through a lp, insert hook in next st,) rep from * leaving lps on the hook.

Do not turn.

Row 2 Yrh, draw through a lp *(yrh draw through 2 lps), rep from * to end of row, 1 ch.

Rep from Row 1, inserting the hook under the vertical thread from right to left, drawing through a lp.

Note To change colour for Row 1, change at the end of Row 2, the last 2 lps, draw contrast through 2 lps.

To cast off, work to end of Row 2. 1 ch, insert hook in the 2nd lp from hook, yrh, draw through 2 lps *(insert hook in next lp, yrh draw through 2 lps) rep from * to end of row. Fasten off.

Make 40 ch.

Work 150 rows (77 patts) simple Tunisian stitch.

Cast off, do not break yarn.

Fold in half, join tog, ss loosely 1 lp each side tog evenly to fold of cushion (2 ss in corners). Ss in each lp bottom edge.

Then join side to top of cushion, leave cover open. Work across the top side of front of you in patt. *(3 ch, ss into back of each st), rep from * all rnd, to beg. Fasten off.

Insert the cushion through open end, stitch together leaving a short end of yarn to tuck in the corner to pull for the cover to be washed.

18. Tunisian Rug

Size

Length including fringe 137cm (54in). Width 76cm (30in).

Materials

17 x red, 4 x Aran 40g balls Lister Lee Aran
10mm Tunisian hook

Tension

6 patts length — 8cm (3in)

Note To change colour for Row 3, join to last 2 sts end of Row 4. Yoh and pull through.

Work with 2 balls tog throughout.
With 10mm Tunisian hook, make 60ch.
Row 1 Insert hook into the top of 2nd ch from hook, yoh and pull through, *(hook into next ch, yoh and pull through). Rep from * to end of row.
Row 2 Yoh, slip 1 st over hook, *(yoh, slip 2 sts over hook). Rep from * ending 1st on hook.
Row 3 *(Insert hook into next lp, yoh and pull through). Rep from * into each lp.
Row 4 Yoh, slip 1 st over hook, *(yoh, slip 2 sts over hook). Rep from * ending 1 st on hook.
Last 2 rows form patt.
Rep last 2 rows until 6 patts have been worked, then Row 3.
***Aran* Work Rows 4 and 3.
Red Work Rows 4 and 3.
Aran Work Rows 4 and 3.
Red Work Row 4, then work 3 patts
Aran Work Rows 3 and 4.
Red Work Rows 3 and 4.
Aran Work Rows 3 and 4.
Red Work 3 patts.
Aran Work Row 3.
Red Work Rows 4 and 3.

Aran Work Rows 4 and 3.
Red Work Rows 4 and 3.
Aran Work Row 4. Break off Aran**.
Red Work Row 3.
Red Work 47 patts.
Red Work Row 3.
Rep patt from ** to **. Break off Aran.
Red Work 6 patts.
Cast off on Row 3, with 1 st on hook. *(Insert hook into next lp, yoh, pull through 2 sts). Rep from * ending 1 st on hook.
Do not break off red. Turn.
Left side 1 dc into back of each lp to bottom edge. 1 dc into each ch st.
Right side as left side. Fasten off.

Fringe

Into back of each dc st – with 2 strands.
Length of strands 13cm (5in)

19. Coat

Size

To fit chest 86cm-91cm (34in-36in). Length from back of neck 96cm (38in)

Materials

10 x 50g balls black, 8 x 50g balls contrast Chanteleine Bidjin, 2 x 100g balls Chanteleine Catimini
10mm Tunisian hook
7.00 crochet hook

Tension

4 rows 3cm (1¼in).

Instructions for stitch

See Simple Tunisian stitch page 53

Note When you change colour for Row 1, change the last 2 lps at the end of Row 2 and draw the contrasting colour through 2 lps.

Back and sleeves all in one

With 10mm Tunisian hook and black yarn make 118 ch.
Work Rows 1 and 2 once.
Change to contrasting colour, work Rows 1 and 2 once.
These 4 rows form patt.
Rep patt until 6 patts length have been worked.
Cast off sleeve with black 34 sts, then Row 1 draw through 50 lps cast off sleeve 34 sts. Break off yarn. Join black yarn to underarm, work Row 2 across 50 sts.

Back

Continue to work patt until 33 patts have been worked from the beg.
   Length can be adjusted. Cast off with black yarn.

Front and sleeves

With black yarn make 47ch.
Work 4 patts, ending with the contrasting colour through 2 lps. Break off yarn.

Shape neck

Left front

With black yarn make 8 ch.
Row 1 Work across 8 ch, continue across 47 sts front (55 sts).
Work Row 2.
Change to contrasting colour and work Rows 1 and 2.
Rep patt, until 6 patts have been worked.
With black yarn patt across 21 sts, cast off sleeve 34 sts.

Join black yarn to underarm and work Row 2, 21 sts, continue to work on these sts until 33 patts from the beg. Cast off in black yarn.

Right front

With black yarn make 47 ch.
Work 4 patts.
Row 1 With black yarn work across 47 sts. Break off yarn.
Make 8 ch. Work Row 1 across 8 ch.
Row 2 With black yarn work across 8 ch, then across 47 sts (55 sts).
Change to contrasting colour and work Rows 1 and 2.
Rep patt until 6 patts have been worked. Break off yarn.
Cast off 34 sts sleeve to underarm.
Continue to work patt, 21 sts front, until 33 patts from beg have been worked. Cast off in black yarn.

Left sleeve

Top of sleeve, match back and front ch st, join with Catimini, 2 strands tog, 7.00 crochet hook at cuff, *(1 dc in front and back ch st tog) rep from * to neck. Fasten off.

Right sleeve

As left sleeve, start from neck to cuff.

Borders

Work 2 balls (2 strands) tog with Catimini.

Cuffs

Rnd 1 Right side of work, with 7.00 hook, 1 dc evenly rnd edge. Ss to 1st dc, turn. 1 ch.
Rnd 2 1 dc in each dc to end of rnd. Ss to join. Fasten off.

Bottom edge

Right side of work, join with 7.00 hook to left corner (1 dc in each st loosely, to right corner 3, dc). (Right front continues 1 dc in each colour to neck, 3 dc.) (Dc rnd neck evenly to left corner of neck, 3 dc.) (Left front as right front to bottom edge, 3 dc.) Ss in next dc, turn, 1 ch.
Rnd 1 With 10mm hook. Left side, 1 dc in each dc (neck, dec at 4 corners). 1 dc in each dc , miss 1 dc in each corner. Right front as left front.
Bottom edge, 1 dc in each dc, ss to 1st dc, turn, 1 ch.
Rep 1st Rnd 6 more times, then 2 rnds, no dec at neck. Fasten off.
Turn border in half wrong side (pin in to shape neck). Sew hem loosely.

20. Hat

Size

Average

Materials

1 x 50g ball black, 1 x 50g ball contrast, Chanteleine Bidjin, 1 x 100g ball Chanteleine Catimini
10mm Tunisian hook

Tension

4 rows 3cm (1¼in)

Note When you change colour for Row 1, change at the end of Row 2, the last 2 lps, draw contrast through 2 lps.

With 10mm Tunisian hook and black wool make 20 ch.
Work Rows 1 and 2 of Simple Tunisian stitch once more.
Change contrast, work Rows 1 and 2 once.
These 4 rows form patt.
Rep patt until 19 patts length have been worked.
Cast off with contrast to top of hat. Break off contrast.
Fold over, wrong side of work, sew side seam with black to top of hat.
Do not break off black. With sewing needle, draw through each lp to beg firmly, then fasten off.

Border

Outside and inside, of Catimini, work with 2 strands tog 10mm hook, right side.
Rnd 1 1 dc loosely in each st to beg. Ss in 1st dc, turn, 1 ch.
Rnd 2 1 dc in each dc to 1st dc, ss to 1 ch.
Rep Rnd 2, 14 times from beg.
Fold over to 1st row, and sew, then fold over once more.

21. Tunisian Bluebell Top

Size

86cm (34in). Size can be adjusted at beg of yoke with number of stitches, with less or more rows, counting rows front and back and armhole, stitches evenly over multiples of 3 sts.

Tunisian framed squares

With white yarn and Tunisian hook, make 16 ch.
Row 1 Insert hook in the 2nd ch from hook * (yrh, draw through a lp, insert hook in next st) rep from * leaving lps on hook.
Do not turn.
Row 2 Yrh, draw through a lp *(yrh, draw through 2 lps) rep from * to end of row.
Rep last 2 rows with blue.
Row 5 *(With white yarn work 2 lps. Yoh, insert hook under vertical lp, in last white row, yoh. Draw through a lp, yoh, draw through 2 lps). Rep from * ending lp to draw through.
Row 6 As Row 2.
Rows 7, 8, 9 and 10 Ts in blue.
Rep last 10 rows to form patt.

Materials

2 x 100g balls blue, 1 x ball white Chanteleine Catimini 100 DK wool
4.50 crochet hook
5.00 Tunisian hook

Tension

4 rows rib – 5cm (2in). 14 rows Tunisian, length over squares 5cm (2in).

Note Draw through loops for half treble evenly, then yoh draw through.

Yoke

With blue yarn and a 4.50 crochet hook make 22 ch.
Row 1 1 hlf tr into 3rd ch from hook, 1 hlf tr in each ch st.
Row 2 2 ch, 1 hlf tr into each hlf tr to end of row.
Rep last row until 78 rows have been worked. Fasten off.
Sew last row to cast on edge. This gives a ribbed yoke.
Right side of work *top* edge: Join the blue yarn.
Rnd 1 1 ch, 1 dc in each row to end of rnd, ss to 1 ch, turn.
Rnd 2 1 ch, 1 dc in each dc, ss to 1 ch. Fasten off, turn.
Join the white yarn, 2 ch.
Rnd 3 1 hlf tr in each dc, ss to top of 2 ch, turn.
Rnd 4 Ss to next sp. Ss in each hlf tr to end of rnd. Fasten off.

Bottom edge of yoke

Join the blue yarn, 1 ch.
Rnd 1 2 dc in each row, ss to 1 ch, turn.
Rnd 2 1 ch, 1 dc in each dc. Ss to 1 ch. Fasten off, turn.
Join the white yarn, 2 ch.

Rnd 3 2 hlf tr in each dc. Ss to top of 2 ch, turn.
Rnd 4 1 ch, 1 dc in each hlf tr. Ss to 1 ch, turn.
Leave 78 sts each side for armholes.

Back (Blue)

Row 1 With 5.00 Tunisian hook, draw lp between each dc st (78 lps).
Row 2 Ts back.
Row 3 Draw through 78 lps.
Row 4 As Row 2.
Work Tunisian framed squares.
White Ts 2 rows (1 patt).
Blue Ts 2 rows (1 patt).
White *(Draw through 2 blue lps, 1 tr into next white horizontal lp) rep from * ending 2 blue lps.
Work 1 row back.
Blue Ts 4 rows (2 patts).
White Ts 2 rows (1 patt).
Blue Ts 2 rows (1 patt).
White *(Draw through 2 blue lps, 1 tr into next white horizontal lp) rep from * ending 2 blue lps.
Work 1 row back.
The last 10 rows complete the patt.
Rep the patt 5 times more, or required length.
Then Ts blue 4 rows (2 patts).
Join the white yarn with the 4.50 crochet hook make 1 ch.
Row 1 1 dc in each lp, 1 ch.
Row 2 1 dc in each dc. Fasten off.

Front

As Back.
Sew side seams to arm.

22. Ironbridge Tunisian Top

Size

91cm–96cm (36in–38in)

Materials

5 x 50g balls main colour, 1 ball contrast Loweth Shetland DK wool
5.00 Tunisian hook, 3.50 crochet hook

Tension

4 sts – 3cm (1in)

Instructions

See Simple Tunisian stitch on page 53.

Front and back alike

With main colour and Tunisian hook make 72 ch.
Work 104 rows of Simple Tunisian stitch (52 patts) to arm.

Arm shaping

Row 1 Cast off 5 sts, Ts to last 5 sts, cast off, break off wool.
Row 2 Join wool, Ts patt back.
Row 3 1 st on hook. (Ts 2 tog) Ts to last 3 sts (Ts 2 tog) 1 Ts.
Row 4 Rep last 2 rows until 52 sts remain.
Work 32 rows Ts (16 patts).

Left shoulder

Row 1 Ts 14 sts.
Row 2 Ts.
Rep last 2 rows 12 times (24 patts). Fasten off.
Join wool, front cast off neck edge, 24 sts, continue to work on 14 sts.
Right shoulder as left.

Front

With contrasting wool work from the chart (figure 28) in cr st, before sewing 2 sides tog, then sew shoulders.

Borders

Armhole and neck edge

With 3.50 crochet hook dc rnd edge, then 1 row, dc in back of sts. Fasten off.

Bottom edge

3 rows rnd dc. Fasten off.

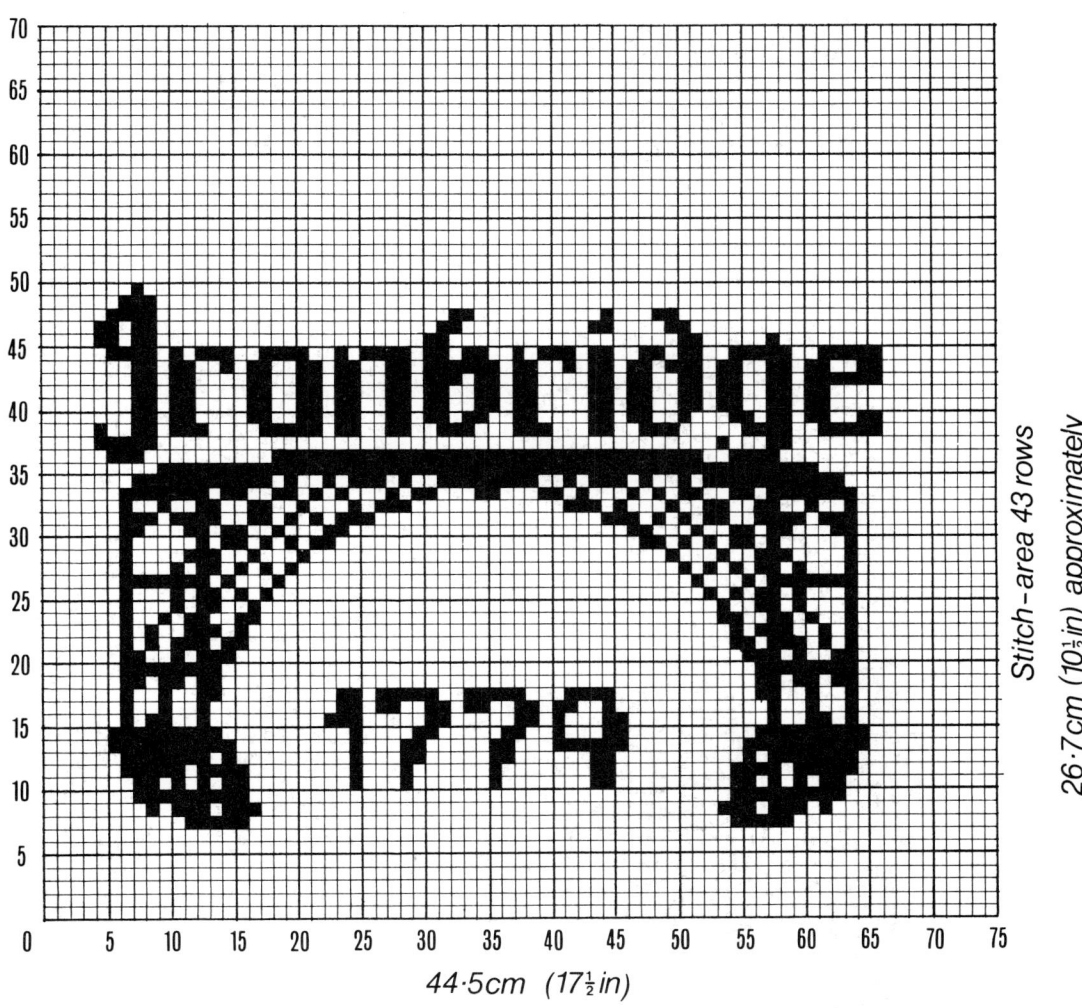

Stitch – area 43 rows

26·7cm (10½in) approximately

44·5cm (17½in)

75 stitches at 4 stitches per 1"

23. Ironbridge Tunisian Sweater

Size

91cm–96cm (36in–38in)

Materials

10 x 50g balls main colour, 1 ball of contrasting colour Loweth Shetland DK wool
5.00 Tunisian hook, 3.50 crochet hook

Tension

4 sts – 3cm (1 in)

Instructions

See Simple Tunisian stitch on page 53.

Front and back

With main colour and Tunisian hook, make 80 ch.
Make 110 rows Ts (55 patts) length to arm.
Arm shaping
Row 1 1 st on hook. (Ts 2 tog) Ts to last 3 sts (Ts 2 tog) 1 Ts.
Rows 2 to 6 Ts.
Rep last 6 rows until 56 sts remain. Cast off.
With contrasting wool work from the chart (figure 28) in cr st before sewing tog.

Sleeves

With main colour, make 67 ch.
Work 120 rows Ts (60 patts) length.
Arm shaping
Dec as front until 49 sts remain.
Shape top of sleeve.
Rows 1 to 5 Ts.
Row 6 1 st on hook (Ts 2 tog) (4 Ts, Ts 2 tog) 3 times. 2 Ts (Ts 3 tog). 2 Ts (Ts 2 tog, 4 Ts) 3 times. (Ts 2 tog) 1 Ts.
Rows 7 to 9 Ts.

Row 10 1 st on hook. (Ts 2 tog.) (3 Ts, Ts 2 tog) 3 times. 3 Ts (Ts 2 tog, 3 Ts) 3 times. (Ts 2 tog) 1 Ts.
Rows 11 to 13 Ts.
Row 14 1 st on hook. (Ts 2 tog) (2 Ts, Ts 2 tog) 3 times. 1 Ts (Ts 2 tog) 3 times. (Ts 2 tog) 1 Ts.
Rows 15 to 17 Ts.
Row 18 1 st on hook. (Ts 2 tog) (1 Ts, Ts 2 tog) twice. 1 Ts (Ts 3 tog). 1 Ts (Ts 2 tog, 1 Ts) twice. (Ts 2 tog) 1 Ts.
Rows 19 to 21 Ts.
Row 22 1 st on hook. (Ts 2 tog) 3 times. 1 Ts (Ts 2 tog) 3 times. 1 Ts.
Row 23 Ts. Cast off.
Sew back and front tog then sew in sleeves.

Borders

Note Dc is worked in the back of each dc st.
Work sleeves and bottom edge with 3.50 crochet hook. Work 10 rnds dc. Fasten off.

Neck

Work 5 rnds dc.
Rnd 6 Dc, miss every 10th dc.
Rnd 7 Dc.
Rnd 8 Dc, miss every 9th dc.
Rnd 9 Dc. Fasten off.

24. Tunisian Sweater and Top

Instructions are the same as for the Ironbridge sweater and top just omit the cross stitch.

Many other designs can be worked in a cross stitch, names, flowers etc.

Suppliers

Aero Needles Group plc
Box No 2 Edward Street
Reddich
Worcestershire B97 6HB
Needles etc

Drawhurst
The Barn
The Butts
Sandwich
Kent CT13 9HX
Needles

Chanteleine
6 Butts Court
Leeds
West Yorkshire LS1 5JX

Debenhams
Buttons

Emu Wools Ltd
Leeds Road
Greengates
Bradford
West Yorkshire BD10 9TE

Lister Handknitting
George Lee & Sons Ltd
Whiteoak

Loweth Wools Ltd
PO Box
140 North Mills
Frog Island
Leicester LE3 5AG

Priory Yarns
24 Prospect Road
Ossett
West Yorkshire WF5 8AE

Dicken & Jones
Regent Street
London
Buttons

Vicars & Poirson Ltd
263-269 City Road
London EC1V 1NT
Handbag handles etc

Roger Underhill
Wedding Specialist
Flower Shop
6a Tontine Hill
The Wharfage
Ironbridge
Shropshire
Bridal decorations

Harrods Ltd
Knightsbridge
London SW1